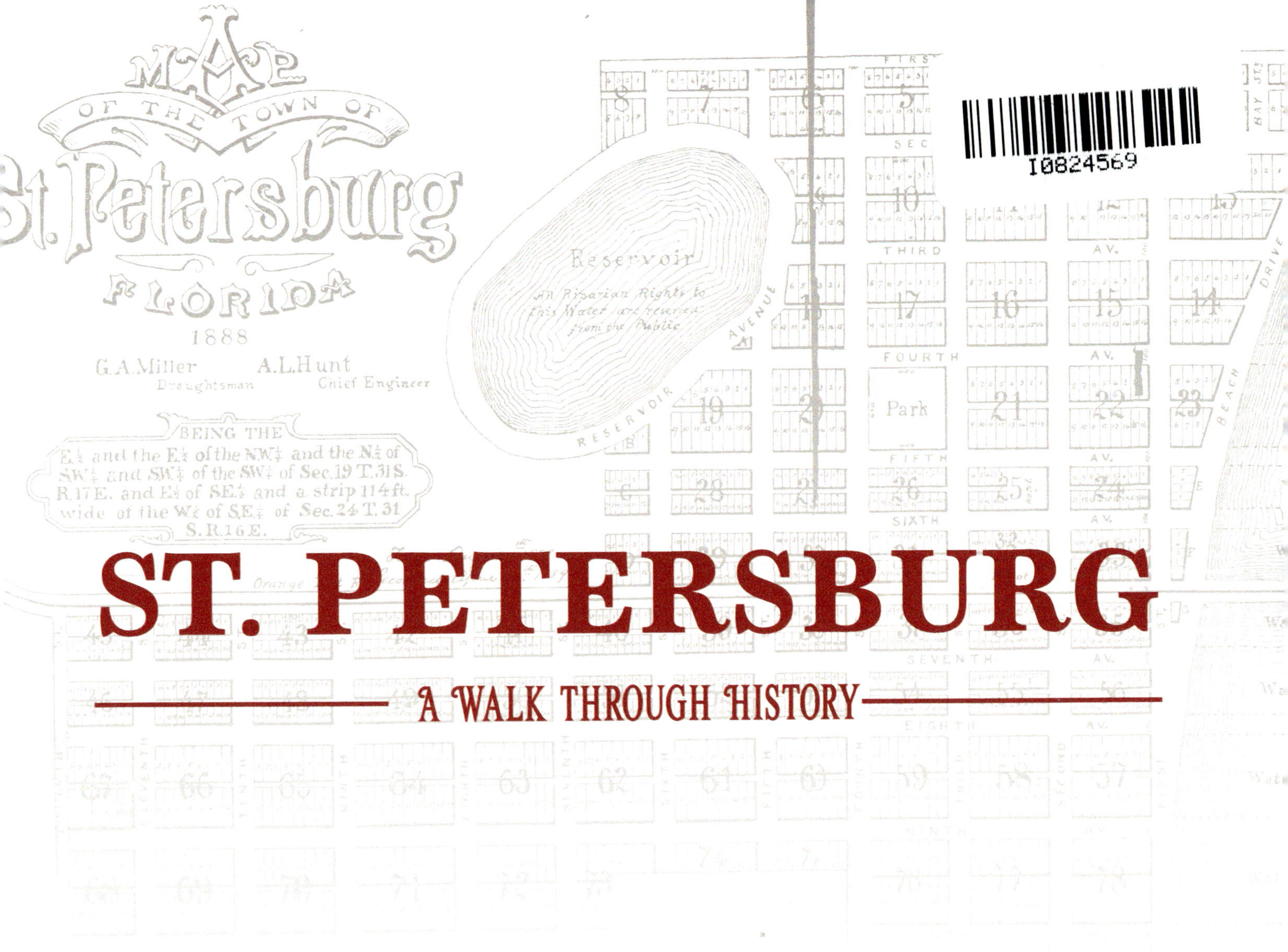

ST. PETERSBURG

A WALK THROUGH HISTORY

Monica Kile

Reedy Press
PO Box 5131
St. Louis, MO 63139
www.reedypress.com

Main front cover photo courtesy of: City of St. Petersburg
Front cover inset images courtesy of (l to r): Tampa-Hillsborough County Public Library System, City of St. Petersburg, City of St. Petersburg, Library of Congress Prints and Photographs Division, Tampa-Hillsborough County Public Library System

Design: Richard Roden

All images are courtesy of the author unless otherwise noted.

ISBN: 9781681065632

Printed in the United States

24 25 26 27 28 5 4 3 2 1

TABLE OF CONTENTS

PANORAMIC VIEW OF ST. PETERSBURG FROM THE LA PLAZA THEATRE
LIBRARY OF CONGRESS

INTRODUCTION

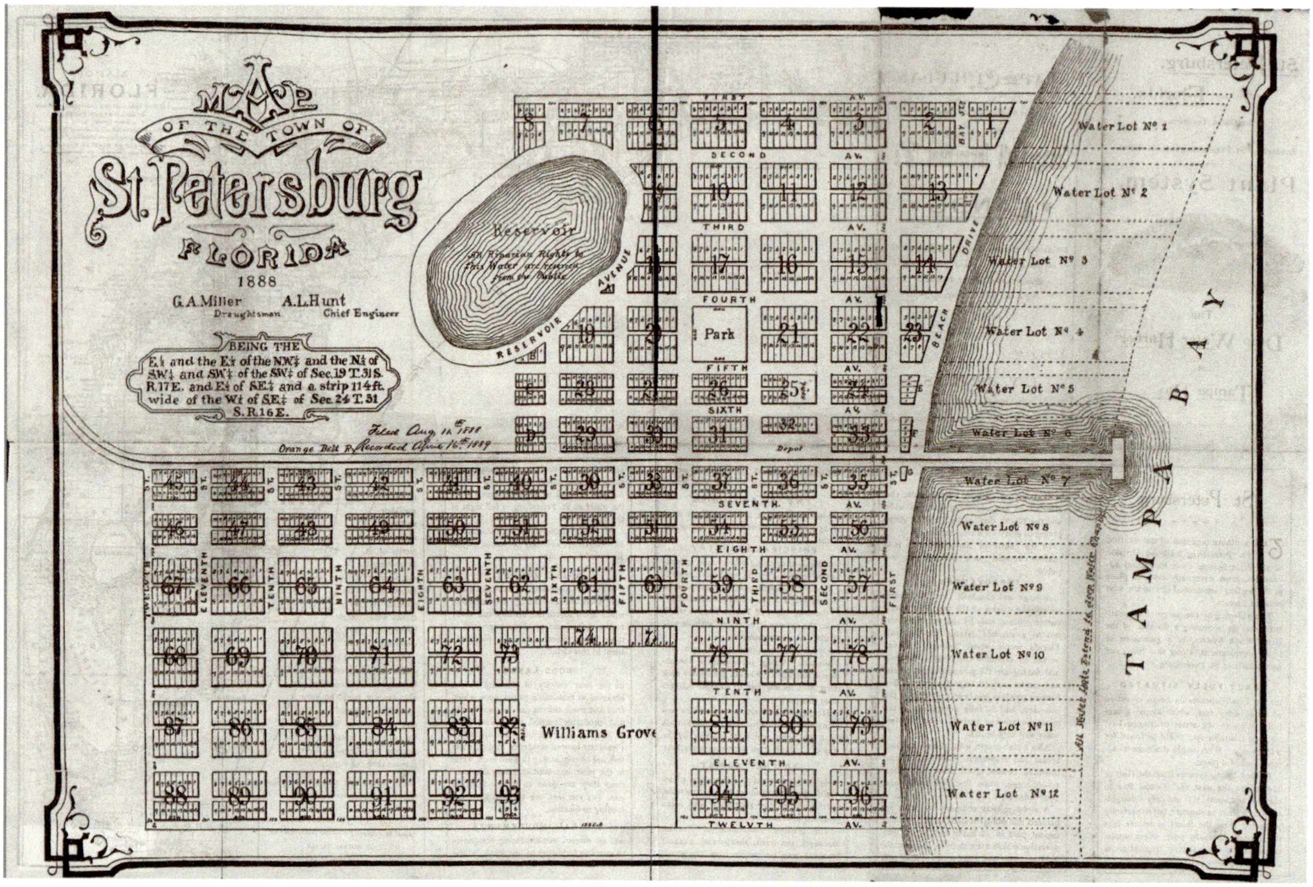

MAP OF ST. PETERSBURG CA. 1888. STATE ARCHIVES OF FLORIDA

St. Petersburg is special. You hear it all the time from residents and visitors alike. There's just something about St. Pete that distinguishes it from other Florida cities, and throughout its history, St. Petersburg has drawn people here from other places. With 361 days of sunshine a year, its appeal seems obvious. But there's more to it than sunshine. There's a character and a charm that is lacking in many Sunbelt cities, a sense of place that is almost tangible.

Because it was developed largely in the 1920s, St. Petersburg has avoided the sprawling fate of most postwar Florida cities. Its downtown is compact and walkable, and many of its original buildings remain intact. Having survived an attempt to raze much of its historic downtown in the 1990s, St. Petersburg has managed a renaissance unlike any other Florida destination over the past 30 years. It has done so by embracing its authenticity and its individuality. Where else can you find the World's Largest Shuffleboard Club? Miles of publicly owned waterfront parkland? Neighborhoods of majestic oak trees shading brick-lined streets and hexagon-block sidewalks? Block upon block of hip art galleries, trendy boutiques, and craft breweries? St. Petersburg has a distinct identity and embraces it.

HISTORY

The land where St. Petersburg grew was originally inhabited by the thriving Native American culture of the Tocobaga Indians, whose societies were decimated by disease following Spanish contact in the 1500s. Later, White American pioneers were given generous land grants in the area if they agreed to fight the Seminole Indians who had migrated to the Tocobaga's former lands. John and William Bethell were two of the pioneers who created a bustling community called Pinellas Village, on the shores of Big Bayou near today's Driftwood neighborhood, where they harvested mullet and shellfish. The village featured a post office, a small hotel, and a general store. Among their nearby neighbors were John and Anna Donaldson, the first African American couple to call the area home.

In the late 1870s a wealthy Detroit native named John C. Williams, in search of a geographic solution to his chronic asthma, purchased 1,600 acres in the area. He was later approached by Russian immigrant Pyotr Demenschev, or Peter Demens, who was looking for land for the terminus of his fledgling Orange Belt Railroad out of Central Florida. Negotiations were clinched by the persuasion skills of Williams's young wife, Sarah, and Demens agreed to bring the railroad to Williams's property rather than to other land being offered in the area. The first Orange Belt train rolled into town on June 8, 1888.

The city's exotically foreign name was inspired by the Russian hometown of Peter Demens. As a concession to city cofounder John Williams, Demens built a grand hotel across from the passenger depot and named it the Detroit Hotel for Williams's hometown. It remains standing today.

In its earliest years, St. Petersburg was largely a fishing community, exporting some three million pounds of fish per year via the railroad and the large sailboats that docked at the Railroad Pier at the foot of today's First Avenue South. Soon, however, the city discovered its true calling when the Orange Belt Railroad began advertising the city as a summer destination for Floridians looking to escape the stifling heat of Central Florida. St. Petersburg offered cool coastal breezes, fishing excursions, and even a toboggan slide at the foot of the railroad pier.

It didn't take long for wealthy northerners looking for a healthy escape from cold and dirty northern cities to begin to call St. Petersburg their winter home. Their choice of the city was undoubtedly influenced by an article published in the *Journal of the American Medical Association*, which proclaimed the area to be the healthiest place in America due to its location—a peninsula on a peninsula. The article was distributed in the waiting rooms of doctors' offices throughout the country. The city's narrative was born: St. Petersburg was a land of sunshine, warmth, and good health. (In the city's first, but certainly not last, example of self-interested boosterism, both the author of the article and the publisher of the journal owned property in the area.)

Over the next few decades St. Petersburg would grow rapidly, thanks in large part to endless promotion. Speculators gobbled up land in the years prior to World War I, and the entire state boomed following the conclusion of the war. The decade of the 1920s saw the city's population increase from 14,000 to 40,000 people (and far more in the winter months). African American

workers were recruited from nearby southern states to help build the roads, seawalls, and other infrastructure of the growing city, leading to the growth of neighborhoods like the Gas Plant and the Deuces. Segregation of the Black population was the norm.

A new architectural style caught on, and soon scores of Mediterranean Revival hotels, churches, and homes dotted the city, allowing residents and visitors to enjoy the luxury and beauty of the Mediterranean without ever leaving the shores of the United States. During the boom, 10 large masonry hotels were built in or around the city, increasing the inventory of hotel rooms from fewer than 500 to nearly 3,000. Of the 10 boom-era hotels, eight are still standing, and five are featured in this book.

The Florida Land Boom went bust in 1926, and the city squeaked through the Great Depression on the dollars of tourists and spring-training fans. During the tense years of World War II, virtually all of the city's major hotels were occupied by soldiers brought to Florida to train in the year-round sun. Many of those soldiers would return following the war, charmed by the Sunshine City like so many others before them.

The real estate and construction boom that followed World War II was unprecedented. Some 47,000 houses were built in the city during the decade of the 1950s, abetted by technological advancements including air-conditioning and DDT. Suburban neighborhoods and adjacent shopping centers blossomed, while the downtown core suffered from a lack of parking and a surplus of aging residents living in newly built, government-subsidized high-rises and the city's old tourist apartments.

While St. Petersburg had long been known as a haven for older people (see Ring Lardner's satirical 1922 story, "The Golden Honeymoon," about a couple visiting the city to celebrate their 50th wedding anniversary) in the decades after 1950, the jokes about the city's elderly population became downright derisive. Among St. Petersburg's nicknames were "God's Waiting Room," "World's Largest Above-ground Cemetery," and "Home of the Newly Wed and the Nearly Dead" (the newly wed being the returning soldiers and their wives). National periodicals commented on the blood-pressure machines on street corners and ambulances running like taxis.

City leaders, eager to revitalize St. Petersburg's image, tore out its famous green benches (long a symbol of hospitality to White visitors, but a painful reminder of inequality for its Black residents, who were not allowed to sit on them). In the late 1980s and early 1990s, they went a step further and proposed tearing down large swaths of downtown to build a shopping complex called Bay Plaza.

Fortunately for today's residents and visitors, cooler heads (and a cooling economy) prevailed, and the Bay Plaza plan dissolved before too much of the historic downtown could be demolished. However, a companion project to build a baseball stadium obliterated the Gas Plant area, a historically African American neighborhood once located adjacent to downtown; echoes of that injustice still resonate in city politics and culture today.

After years of trying to revive the city by remaking it into something new, what followed was a renaissance based almost exclusively on the celebration of classic St. Petersburg: the renovation of the historic Vinoy Hotel, the revitalization of the Shuffleboard Club, and the construction of high-rise condos with views overlooking the city's world-class, publicly owned, waterfront park system. St. Petersburg has once again discovered that the best product it can sell is itself.

These eight walking tours will show you some of the historic highlights of St. Petersburg and tell the city's unique story. They are mostly located in or near downtown, with one tour a little farther south to highlight the historically African American main street of the Deuces neighborhood. There are many other historic neighborhoods in the city that will hopefully make it into a future volume of *St. Petersburg: A Walk through History*.

Creating walking tour routes can be tricky and somewhat arbitrary. A visitor would be well served to read through all of the tours before embarking in order to more efficiently plan their day. The tours are designed to show off the city's most beautiful and interesting buildings, as well as some of the more utilitarian structures where the city's everyday citizens carried out the work that has always made St. Petersburg such a wonderful place to live and to visit. Enjoy!

ST. PETERSBURG IS A TOTALLY MODERN CITY THAT ALSO EMBRACES ITS PAST.

TOUR ONE
THE SCENIC WATERFRONT
7th Ave. NE
6th Ave. NE
5th Ave. NE
4th Ave. NE
3rd Ave. NE
2nd Ave. NE
Sunshine Ln.
1st Ave. NE
1st Ave. S
1st Ave. SE
2nd St. N
1st St. N
2nd St. S
1st St. S
Beach Dr. NE
Bayshore Dr. NE
Bayshore Dr. SE
North Straub Park
South Straub Park
Pioneer Park
Demens Landing Park
North Yacht Basin
Central Yacht Basin
South Yacht Basin
1
2
3
4
5
6
7
8
9
10
11
12
13

TOUR ONE

THE SCENIC WATERFRONT

Approximately 1.6 miles

The stunning vistas and myriad entertainments of St. Petersburg's waterfront have drawn visitors for decades, but this destiny was not a foregone conclusion. The downtown coastline was transformed from a gritty, working waterfront in the early 20th century by local boosters who had a vision of St. Petersburg as a "city beautiful."

You'll find a historic marker at the foot of the bridge to Demens Landing, where First Avenue Southeast meets Bayshore Drive Southeast. From there you can observe the first two stops on this tour.

1 Demens Landing/ The South Mole

Intersection of 1st Ave. SE and Bayshore Dr. SE

This is the location of the city's first pier, built in 1889, where freight was transferred between the Orange Belt Railroad and large ships. Residents also used the pier for swimming, and it featured an attractive bathhouse and slide. Eventually, recreational activities were moved to the municipal pier at Second Avenue North after its construction in 1913.

For many years the area adjacent to the railroad pier, known as the South Mole, was used as a bathing beach for African Americans, one of the only places where Black residents could swim legally. The rail lines and pier were removed in 1963 and the land sold to the city. It was turned into a park in 1977.

STATE ARCHIVES OF FLORIDA

While standing at the Demens Landing historic marker, look across the street and to the southwest to see Al Lang Stadium.

2 Al Lang Stadium and Spring Training

230 1st St. SE

Baseball's spring training played a defining role in St. Petersburg's history for over a century. Al Lang Stadium is named for the Pennsylvania transplant who convinced the St. Louis Browns to hold spring training here in 1914. The following year the Philadelphia Phillies trained here and went on to win the National League pennant, raising the city's profile in the baseball world (and leading to Lang's election as mayor). There has been a stadium in this general location since 1921, which over the years was the spring home of the Boston Braves, the St. Louis Cardinals, and the biggest legends to play for the New York Yankees, from Babe Ruth to Joe DiMaggio to Mickey Mantle. The present stadium was built in 1977 and is now used by the Tampa Bay Rowdies soccer team.

CITY OF ST. PETERSBURG

Cross to the northwest corner of First Avenue Southeast and Bayshore Drive and head diagonally through Pioneer Park with its 20-foot-high obelisk displaying the names of early civic leaders. Come out at the southeast corner of Central Avenue and Beach Drive, across from

the Bayfront Tower, downtown's first high-rise condo, built in 1975. On the northwest corner you'll see the Ponce de Leon Hotel.

3 Ponce de Leon Hotel
95 Central Ave.

The Ponce de Leon has operated as a hotel almost continuously since 1922, the first major hotel built along the waterfront. Designed by notable local architect George Feltham, who also designed the First Baptist Church and the Green-Richman Arcade, the hotel housed a steady stream of tourists, baseball players, and World War II soldiers. President Richard Nixon stayed here, as did actor Christopher Reeve. During the Bay Plaza period, the hotel was closed for several years and slated for demolition, but it was later renovated and reopened. It is a local historic landmark.

TAMPA-HILLSBOROUGH COUNTY PUBLIC LIBRARY SYSTEM

Walk north on Beach Drive one block. Cross First Avenue North and then go west on First Avenue North and walk a half block to the historic sign on the street.

4 Soreno Hotel Fountain
100 Beach Dr. NE (marker is on the south side of the Florencia condominium facing 1st Ave. N)

A fountain on the side of the Florencia condominium is all that remains of the grand Soreno Hotel. Built by Danish immigrant Soren Lund, it opened on New Year's Eve 1924. Lund named the hotel after his son; *Soreno* basically means "little Soren." Well-heeled patrons spent the entire winter season here, enjoying the coffee shop on the fifth floor and putting golf balls in the park across the street. The aging hotel operated until 1984, when it could no longer meet fire codes. It was demolished in 1992, over tremendous local resistance, as part of the Bay Plaza plan to redevelop downtown. (The comparable Vinoy Hotel reopened that same year.) The demolition earned St. Pete 15 minutes of fame when it was featured in the closing credits of the movie *Lethal Weapon 3*. You can see the Soreno Hotel in the background of the Yacht Club photo on this page.

Return to Beach Drive and cross over to the park. Walk diagonally through the park to the northeast corner, where Second Avenue Northeast meets Bayshore Drive. As you walk, you'll pass the St. Petersburg Yacht Club on your right before ending up at a historic marker commemorating William Straub.

5 St. Petersburg Yacht Club
11 Central Ave.

The Yacht Club was originally founded in 1909, and this building was constructed in 1917. Because it is located on city-owned parkland, a 1917 dispute over the legality of the club's lease had to be settled by the Florida legislature. In 1921, the worst hurricane to ever hit St. Petersburg flooded the Yacht Club and much of downtown. From 1930 to 1959, the club sponsored a popular boat race from St. Petersburg to Havana, Cuba.

TAMPA-HILLSBOROUGH COUNTY PUBLIC LIBRARY SYSTEM

6 South Straub Park

Historic Marker: Southwest Corner of 2nd Ave. NE and Bayshore Dr.

Originally named Waterfront Park in 1910, the first unit of the city's famous park system was renamed Straub Park in 1939 after William Straub, the influential owner and editor of the *St. Petersburg Times*, who moved to the city in 1899 for health reasons. Straub believed that the city's working waterfront should be beautified for the sake of residents and visitors. A tireless booster, Straub successfully advocated for public ownership of the waterfront, and in 1910, work began on what would become one of the largest public waterfronts in North America—currently more than seven miles in total.

CITY OF ST. PETERSBURG

From the historic marker on the southwest corner of Second Avenue Northeast and Bayshore Drive, cross to the northeast corner to view the small octagonal brick building. This is the Comfort Station.

7 The Comfort Station

Northeast Corner of 2nd Ave. NE and Bayshore Dr. NE

The city's most beautiful public restroom, this Romanesque Revival–style building was designed by architect Henry Taylor in 1927. Local legend claims that Taylor modeled the bathroom after St. Mary's Catholic Church after they failed to pay him for designing their new sanctuary. Locals therefore know the bathroom by its nickname of "Little St. Mary's." Alas, the Comfort Station was built in 1927, while the church was not erected until 1930, so the tale is likely just a confection to amuse tourists. The building is a local historic landmark.

MONICA KILE

From the Comfort Station, walk east on the pier. After passing the outdoor market kiosks, you will come upon a large aerial sculpture that resembles a giant net. On the north side is Spa Beach, and to the south you will see a full-sized metal sculpture of a biplane. Take your time and explore these and other pier sites.

8 The Pier

2nd Ave. NE and Bayshore Dr. NE

As part of its newfound dedication to city beautification and the burgeoning tourism industry, the city built a municipal recreation pier here in 1913. After the 1921 hurricane damaged the first pier, a new "Million Dollar Pier" opened to great fanfare on Thanksgiving Day 1926 with 10,000 spectators there to celebrate. The 1,400- foot-long pier boasted a swimming area, a solarium, a bait house, a streetcar line, and a spectacular Mediterranean Revival–style casino with a ballroom and observation deck. Time took its toll, however, and the iconic Million Dollar Pier was demolished in 1967 and the innovative "inverted pyramid" pier opened in 1973. That pier was demolished in 2015 and the popular new St. Pete Pier opened in 2021.

CITY OF ST. PETERSBURG

9 Spa Beach
North Side of the Pier

Spa Beach was once home to a pool and so-lar-ium, the latter featuring an en-trance resem-bling an Egyptian tem-ple and tall, concrete walls that protected nude sun-bathers from the gaze of passersby. The beach and pool were originally off-limits to Black residents. In the late 1950s, African American residents filed a lawsuit and staged swim-ins to protest the segregation policy, leading the city manager to close the beach and pool for months at a time. Eventually, downtown businesses complained about the impact on tourism, and both the pool and beach were quietly desegregated. The nearby *Bending Arc* aerial sculpture by Janet Echelman was named in tribute to these civil rights activities. The name comes from a Martin Luther King Jr. quote, "The arc of the moral universe is long, but it bends toward justice."

10 Central Yacht Basin and the First Flight
South Side of the Pier

On New Year's Day 1914, the world's first airline was launched from here when pilot Tony Jannus flew a seaplane from St. Petersburg's Central Yacht Basin to downtown Tampa for the St. Petersburg–Tampa Airboat Line. It was the first commercial airline flight in the world. Tickets were five dollars each way, and two flights a day were flown for three months before the airline folded for lack of revenue. An impressive memorial is located on the pier, featuring a life-size sculpture of the Benoist Airplane and its passengers in the exact spot of the airline's original hangar.

Take all the time you need to explore the pier, with its restaurants, aquarium, splash pad, and playground. The tram is free and runs continually. When you are done, retrace your steps back to Bayshore Drive (or ride the tram to the pier's western terminus). Cross Bayshore Drive and go one block west to Beach Drive and make a right. Note the large tree on the right as you make your way to the Museum of Fine Arts.

11 Museum of Fine Arts
255 Beach Dr. NE

The Museum of Fine Arts opened in 1965 with funding from a wealthy heiress. The museum was actually given ownership of 4.5 acres of the city's waterfront parkland on the condition that the building would always be used as an art museum and the grounds would always remain open to the public. A 2008 addition doubled the museum's size. Its collection covers 5,000 years of art and features French artists like Monet and Rodin along with contemporary artists. The impressive kapok tree on the south side of the building was just a few feet tall when it was planted in 1965, the year the museum opened. It features stunning red blooms in late winter.

The banyan trees near the Museum of Fine Arts are a type of ficus that is native to India. The first banyan tree was imported to Florida in 1925 by tire businessman Harvey Firestone as a gift to Thomas Edison at his Fort Myers winter home.

Continue along Beach Drive, passing two large banyan trees. After passing the second banyan tree, pause and look across Beach Drive and note the Birchwood Inn with its restaurant and rooftop bar.

12 Lantern Lane Apartments
340 Beach Dr. NE

In 1924, the Lantern Lane Apartments were built by May Purnell, an early female developer. In 2012, the building underwent a substantial rehabilitation, including the addition of two floors, to become the hotel, restaurant, and bar you see today. At that time it was also designated as a local historic landmark.

CITY OF ST. PETERSBURG

Continue north on Beach Drive, and then cut diagonally through North Straub Park (passing a headless statue on your right) until you reach the corner of Bayshore Drive and Fifth Avenue Northeast. In front of you is the famous Vinoy Park Hotel.

TAMPA-HILLSBOROUGH COUNTY PUBLIC LIBRARY SYSTEM

13 Vinoy Park Hotel
501 5th Ave. NE

The jewel of the waterfront, the Vinoy Park Hotel opened on New Year's Eve 1925. It was built by Pennsylvania millionaire Aymer Vinoy Laughner and designed by architect Henry L. Taylor. In its day it hosted the DuPonts, the Guggenheims, the Pillsburys, Babe Ruth, and F. Scott Fitzgerald.

The hotel is a wonderful example of Mediterranean Revival architecture (or Med Rev for short) featuring many arches, balconies, and a barrel-tile roof, along with Florida limestone around the entryway and a textured stucco exterior.

During World War II, soldiers from the Army Air Forces Technical Training Center were quartered here. Following decades of decline, the Vinoy Hotel closed in 1975 and remained boarded up until 1992, when it was renovated and reopened to great fanfare.

The Waterfront Tour concludes here. If you still have energy, the Residential Downtown Tour begins not far from here.

DID YOU KNOW?

The five sculptures of human figures that dot North Straub Park were brought here in the 1920s by developer Perry Snell, who imported dozens of Italian sculptures to line the neighborhoods he built. After some of the sculptures were vandalized, Snell moved them into more visible parks in the city, like these in North Straub Park.

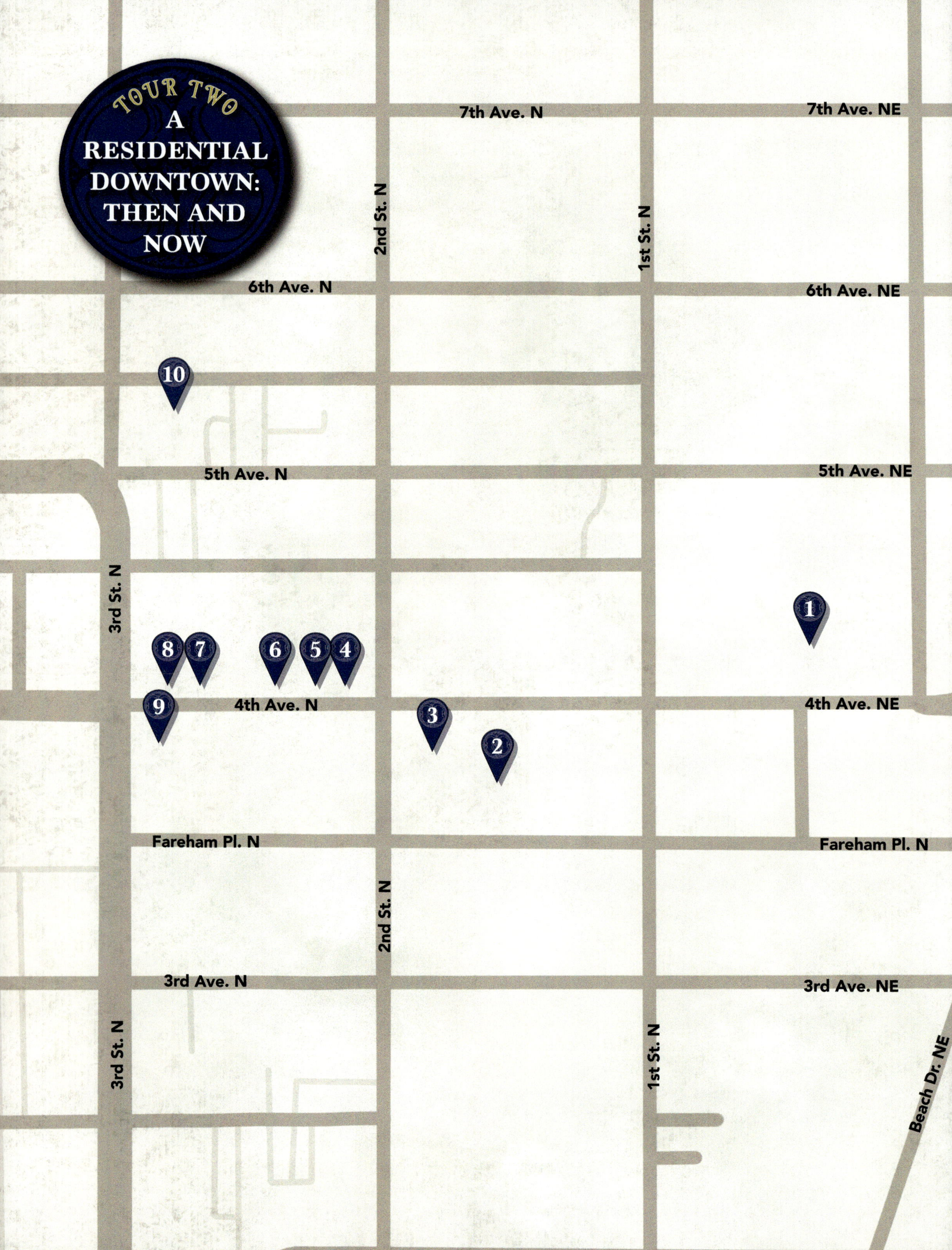
TOUR TWO
A RESIDENTIAL DOWNTOWN: THEN AND NOW
7th Ave. N
7th Ave. NE
2nd St. N
1st St. N
6th Ave. N
6th Ave. NE
10
5th Ave. N
5th Ave. NE
3rd St. N
1
8
7
6
5
4
9
4th Ave. N
3
4th Ave. NE
2
Fareham Pl. N
Fareham Pl. N
2nd St. N
3rd Ave. N
3rd Ave. NE
3rd St. N
1st St. N
Beach Dr. NE

TOUR TWO

A RESIDENTIAL DOWNTOWN: THEN AND NOW

Approximately 0.4 miles

In St. Pete's earliest years, winter visitors built grand estates downtown. As the city boomed in the 1920s and 1950s and large hotels were built, many of these grand homes were subdivided into guesthouses or retirement homes, or demolished. This tour will take you past what remains of St. Petersburg's original downtown housing stock.

Start this tour at 145 Fourth Avenue Northeast. The house in front of you is the Blocker House.

1 Blocker House
145 4th Ave. NE

ST. PETERSBURG MUSEUM OF HISTORY

One of the oldest remaining examples of an early private home in St. Petersburg, this was built as the residence of A.T. and Hattie Blocker in 1905. A.T. was the owner of Blocker's Livery Service, which provided all manner of transportation, from mule teams to buggies to a horse-drawn hearse. Blocker went on to have a successful political career. The house, a beautiful example of a Queen Anne Victorian, was a wedding gift from Hattie's parents, who lived next door. In 1926 the house was purchased by the Shriners and served as a community meeting space for decades.

Go west on Fourth Avenue Northeast and cross First Street North. About midblock, on the south side you will see a seven-story building shaped in a U that forms a courtyard. This is the Flori-de-Leon Cooperative.

2 Flori-de-Leon Cooperative
130 4th Ave. N

MONICA KILE

In the early 1920s, a group of doctors, lawyers, and businessmen who wintered in Florida decided they would prefer to own their own place in St. Petersburg rather than always pay for a hotel. They built what would become one of the first cooperative apartment buildings on Florida's west coast. The striking Med Rev high-rise, built in 1926, featured two penthouse apartments, which were rented in the 1920s and 1930s by legendary baseball players Babe Ruth and Lou Gehrig when they were in town for spring training. The Flori, as locals call it, is a local historic landmark.

Just to the west of the Flori-de-Leon is the former Carleve Hotel. The front of this building faces Second Street, so take a peek around the corner to get the best look.

3 The Carleve Hotel
357 2nd St. N

THE STATE ARCHIVES OF FLORIDA

Built in 1939 this 48-room hotel was called the Carleve Hotel, its name taken from the

first names of its husband-and-wife owners, Carl and Eve Perzina. It operated on the European Plan (guests' stay did not include meals) and its dining room was open to the public. In the 1960s, it converted into a retirement home, and then in 1975 was purchased by the Order of Friars Minor, Franciscan Brotherhood, who continue to operate it today as a retirement home for Franciscan Friars.

Continue west on Fourth Avenue North. On the northwest corner of Second Street and Fourth Avenue North is the Crislip House.

4 Crislip House
205 4th Ave. N

MONICA KILE

The family of John A. Crislip began wintering in St. Petersburg around 1907, eventually buying a home on the 600 block of Central Avenue, across the street from the arcade they would later build and give their name to (see page 19). The Crislips built this home on fashionable Fourth Avenue North in 1923. The house is a classic example of the Mission Revival style (which references Spanish missions), with details like the shaped parapet, wide overhanging eaves, exposed brackets, and prominent front porch.

Moving west, next to the Crislip House is the:

5 Bussey House
211 4th Ave. N

This home, called Palm Villa by its first owner, H.P. Bussey, was moved from its original location at 451 Central Avenue in 1913. Bussey founded the city's first cemetery, Greenwood Cemetery. The home, believed to have been built around 1904, features typical Queen Anne–style elements like the gingerbread trim on the porch.

ST. PETERSBURG MUSEUM OF HISTORY

Next door to the west is the Mount Vernon Hotel.

6 Mount Vernon Hotel
219 4th Ave. N

MONICA KILE

This building was built in 1936 by Mary Carr, whose family were early pioneers in the hotel industry in St. Pete. Within a year, 54 rooms were added. It reopened in November of 1937 as the Mount Vernon Hotel, advertising steam heat, an elevator, and a sundeck on the roof. Each room had a private bath. The hotel was converted into a senior living facility in 1977, and then into condominiums in 2003.

Two doors down from the Mount Vernon are the Sarven Apartments.

7 Sarven Apartments
249 4th Ave. N

MONICA KILE

Constructed in 1921 by George Sarven, this building featured 18 units. A 1922 advertisement cautioned interested renters to "not believe everything you've heard about our high prices." The Classical Revival–style building still serves as apartments today.

Continuing to the northeast corner of Fourth Avenue North and Third Street, you'll find the Davenport House.

8 Davenport House

259 4th Ave. N

Built in 1905 for Mr. and Mrs. W. J. Slemmer of Pennsylvania, this Queen Anne–style residence was called "one of the finest residences in South Florida" by the *St. Petersburg Times*. Slemmer sold the home in 1911 to wealthy banker George Yandes of Indianapolis, who wintered there with his three nieces. (When Yandes died in 1913, his estate was valued at nearly a million dollars, equivalent to $30 million today, and the details of his will were national news.) The home was later converted into a guesthouse and then office space in the 1980s.

On the southeast corner, across from the Davenport House is the Veillard House.

9 Veillard House

262 4th Ave. N

The Veillard House was designed by architect Henry Dupont and built in 1901 by local merchant and civic leader Ralph Veillard. It is a Queen Anne–style bungalow made out of rose-colored rusticated block, an early form of poured concrete that was meant to resemble stone. The house was relocated in 1979 from two blocks west after its potential demolition caused a tremendous community outcry. Preservationist Frances McSwain Pruitt led the charge to save the building, purchasing the lot and arranging for the transfer of the house on the very day it was to be demolished. After its relocation, it was used as offices. It is a local historic landmark.

Turn right on Third Street and walk north one block to Fifth Avenue North. You'll pass several 1920s apartment buildings on the east side of the street, and a 1922 wood-frame, single-family home (now office) on the west. On the northeast corner of Fifth Avenue North and Fourth Street is the First Church of Christ, Scientist/Palladium.

10 First Church of Christ, Scientist/Palladium

253 5th Ave. N

This large Renaissance Revival–style building was built as the First Church of Christ, Scientist, in 1926. Designed by architect Howard Lovewell Cheney (who designed the original terminal at Washington National Airport), it was constructed by the George Fuller Company, builder of New York's Flatiron Building and the Lincoln Memorial. The gorgeous tiles inside came from the California workshop of Ernest Batchelder, an artisan renowned for his Arts and Crafts–style work. Established as a nonprofit performing-arts venue in 1998, the building was renamed the Palladium. It became part of St. Petersburg College in 2007 and was designated a local historic landmark in 2012.

You'll find the popular Kahwa Coffee shop at the corner of Fifth Avenue North and Second Street is a great place to relax at the conclusion of this tour.

TOUR THREE
BUILDING A TOURIST TOWN
7th Ave. N
6th Ave. N
5th Ave. N
4th Ave. N
3rd Ave. N
2nd Ave. N
1st Ave. N
Central Ave. N
Central Ave. N
1st Ave. S
1st Ave. S
Sunshine Ln.
Williams Park
1st St. N
2nd St. N
4th St. N
5th St. N
Beach Dr. NE
5th St. S
4th St. S
3rd St. S
2nd St. S
1st St. S
1
2
3
4
5
6
7
8
9

TOUR THREE
BUILDING A TOURIST TOWN

Approximately 0.5 miles

This tour will give you a great feel for St. Petersburg's early boom years of the 1910s and 1920s.

Start this tour at the Visitors' Center in the Chamber of Commerce building at 100 Second Avenue N.

1 Concord Hotel
100 2nd Ave. N

The Homestead Hotel opened at this location in 1926 and often served as overflow space for the nearby Soreno Hotel. In 1928, it changed names to the Madrid, and then to the Concord Hotel. Later additions doubled its size and added a swimming pool, the only one in a downtown St. Petersburg hotel. In 1985, it was slated for conversion to office space when it was unexpectedly gutted by a major fire. It is now owned in part by the Chamber of Commerce, and includes a visitors' center.

STATE ARCHIVES OF FLORIDA

Cross to the north side of Second Avenue North. On the southwest corner of Second Avenue North and Second Street is the Palais Royal.

2 Palais Royal
146 2nd St. N

Built as the Hartman Amusement Palace in 1926, this Mediterranean Revival–style building was designed by architect George Feltham. It hosted 4,000 people at its inaugural ball. By the fall of 1926, the hall had become known as the Palais Royal (no "e"). In 1929, the building began a stint as the St. Petersburg Tourist Center, a city-managed facility where the state tourist societies met for dances, games, and lectures. The ballroom continued to operate until the late 1960s and was converted to offices in 1985.

MONICA KILE

3 Cordova Hotel
253 2nd Ave. N

When it was constructed in 1921, the mid-size Cordova Hotel was considered quite modern, advertising a telephone, steam heat, and bath with every room. It is Neoclassical Revival style with decorative columns supporting the open, arcaded entrance. Originally called the Hotel Scott, after its owner Frederick Scott, it was renamed the Cordova Hotel in 1924. It is a local historic landmark.

TAMPA-HILLSBOROUGH COUNTY PUBLIC LIBRARY SYSTEM

Continue west and cross Third Street to admire the First United Methodist Church.

4 First United Methodist Church
212 3rd St. N

Construction began on the First United Methodist Church in 1925 but had to begin again the following

TAMPA-HILLSBOROUGH COUNTY PUBLIC LIBRARY SYSTEM

year when the east wall of the church collapsed during construction. Designed in a Gothic Revival style, the church is perhaps most recognized for its striking stained-glass windows, including a re-creation of Da Vinci's *Last Supper*, and its 144-foot-tall bell tower, which houses 15 bells. It was the location of the wedding scene in the 1985 movie *Cocoon*. It is a local historic landmark.

DID YOU KNOW?

A uniquely St. Petersburg phenomenon, the city's first tourist society was organized by winter visitors from Illinois on January 1, 1902. By 1923, practically every state in the country was represented by a tourist society, and membership exceeded 12,000 people. The societies were designed to provide local advice, instant fellowship, and fun. Members served as boosters in their home communities, helping to make St. Petersburg a famous resort city.

Continue west on Second Avenue North and then head north on Third Street. After the first alley, you will see a two-story home on the east side of Third Street. This is the Endicott House/ Stewart Hotel.

5 Endicott House/Stewart Hotel
233 3rd St. N

This ca. 1913 house belonged to real estate agent and undertaker J.M. Endicott who owned the funeral home on Second Avenue South found on page 33.

MONICA KILE

In the 1920s, the home was converted into a boardinghouse, and later the Stewart Hotel. In 1984, it became office space. Notice the large, enclosed second-story porch, which was likely used as a sleeping porch in the days before air-conditioning.

Continue north on Third Street. At the southwest corner of Third Street and Third Avenue North you'll find the Palm Plaza.

6 Palm Plaza
256 3rd St. N

This building was designed by prominent mid-century architect William Harvard. It was built on the lot of the former home of State Representative Charles Schuh Jr., whose house was moved in January of 1950 to make way for the new office building he would share with his father. Tragically, Schuh Jr. was murdered in April of that year, shot by the disgruntled husband of a former client. This building, dedicated in honor of the beloved lawyer and politician, rose the following month. It was lauded in the *St. Petersburg Times* as "one of the most modern designs of the new commercial buildings." Note how the facade of each storefront angles in from the street, and how the terrazzo flooring extends from inside to outside.

MONICA KILE

Turn left on Third Avenue North and walk one block west to Fourth Street. On the northwest corner of Third Avenue North and Fourth Street North is the Pennsylvania Hotel.

7 Pennsylvania Hotel
300 4th St. N

STATE ARCHIVES OF FLORIDA

The Pennsylvania Hotel was built in 1925. It is one of the 10 boom-era hotels, and the building's Chicago-style architecture—blending Art Deco and classical influences—is rare here. Featuring 92 rooms when built, the hotel was renovated and turned into a Marriott in 2005 and expanded with an additional tower. During the renovation, every two rooms in the historic building were combined into one. To keep the hallways historically authentic, every other door is fake. The developers of the tower addition noted that it was not meant to copy the original hotel design but would be like a "great-granddaughter." The original building is a local historic landmark.

Cross Fourth Street. On the southwest corner of Fourth Street and Third Avenue is one of St. Pete's oldest churches, First Congregational Church.

8 First Congregational Church
256 4th St. N

TAMPA-HILLSBOROUGH COUNTY PUBLIC LIBRARY SYSTEM

Built in 1912, this building was designed by Edgar Ferdon, the city's first professional architect. A wonderful example of Gothic Revival architecture, the church was used as a set in the 1979 PBS movie *The Golden Honeymoon* based on the 1920s short story by Ring Lardner. The church and parish hall were sold in 1994 to a developer who turned the parish hall into a private residence. The church is a local historic landmark.

Continue south on Fourth Street North. After passing the alley, you will encounter the Orange Blossom Cafeteria.

9 Orange Blossom Cafeteria
220 4th St. N

ST. PETERSBURG MUSEUM OF HISTORY

Constructed in 1925, this building became the Orange Blossom Cafeteria in 1930. It held on longer than any other downtown cafeteria. When they finally closed the doors in 1986, the owner nearly cried for the long-term patrons he knew would suffer without the beloved cafeteria. Many of them had eaten all of their meals there for nearly 30 years.

The tour concludes here. Consider exploring inside one of the nearby churches, many of which welcome visitors.

DID YOU KNOW?

The radical concept of the cafeteria—an affordable yet elegant restaurant where food was dished out by friendly servers—took St. Petersburg by storm in the 1920s. Catering to winter visitors, the cafeterias engaged in price wars, serving dinner for less than a dollar. The most popular cafeterias served up to 2,000 diners a day. Business began to suffer in the 1960s, and most closed by the 1980s. (See Tramor in the Evolving St. Pete Tour.)

TOUR FOUR
THE "FIRST BLOCK" AND HISTORIC CENTRAL AVENUE
I-375
4th Ave. N
3rd Ave. N
2nd Ave. N
Sunshine Ln
1st Ave. N
Central Ave.
Central Ave
1st Ave. S
2nd Ave. S
3rd Ave. S
4th Ave. S
5th Ave. S
I-175
4th St. N
3rd St. N
2nd St. N
5th St. N
7th St. S
6th St. S
5th St. S
4th St. S
3rd St. S
2nd St. S
Mirror Lake
Mirror Lake Dr.
Williams Park
1
2
3
4
5
6
7
8
9
10
11
12
13
14
15

TOUR FOUR

THE "FIRST BLOCK" AND HISTORIC CENTRAL AVENUE

Approximately 0.8 miles

The buildings on the 200 block of both Central Avenue and First Avenue North are some of the most historic in the city, earning the nickname First Block. You'll also see other Central Avenue landmarks.

Start this tour on the corner of Central Avenue and Second Street.

1 Detroit Hotel

201–215 Central Ave.

The Detroit Hotel is the most historically significant building in St. Petersburg, constructed in 1888 by the Orange Belt Railway. In 1889, the railroad, whose passenger depot was across the street on Central Avenue, began offering summer excursions to St. Petersburg, which included a stay at the 40-room, wood-frame, Queen Anne–style hotel. Visitors from Florida's stifling interior were lured by the coastal city's refreshing sea breezes, starting the city's long history as a resort destination.

Two brick additions were added in 1910 and 1913. Other renovations, which included covering the original wooden building in stucco, have significantly altered its appearance. The hotel closed in 1992 and was later converted into condominiums. If the walls could talk they would tell of visits by Eleanor Roosevelt, John F. Kennedy, Will Rogers, Clarence Darrow, and Ringo Starr, along with hosting a hundred years of important political, civic, and social events in the city. It is a local historic landmark.

Next to the Detroit Hotel is the Michigan Building and the Ramsey Block.

2 Michigan Building and the Ramsey Block

231–245 Central Ave.

Built in 1909, the masonry vernacular structure at 231–235 Central Avenue is known as the Michigan Building after the home state of its developer. The two brick buildings to the west were built by the city's first female developer, Mary Ramsey. They were home to the city's first movie theater, the Royal Palms, which showed silent movies beginning in 1905. The St. Charles Hotel operated on the second floor; you can still see the hotel sign in the brick parapet above the balcony at 245 Central, and a "thirst-quenching emporium" occupied the ground floor (a harbinger of things to come—today, restaurants and bars abound on this block!).

3 Norton Building and Lewis Grocery

259–277 Central Ave.

To the west of the Ramsey Building stands the two-story Norton Building, built in 1906 by James

Norton. The building was covered in cementitious panels in 1966 along with the adjacent buildings to the west, and connected by the metal canopy that now shades the sidewalk. These buildings all featured unique styles, from brick vernacular to Victorian, and were home to a variety of businesses that were essential to Florida's boom, including gift shops, pharmacies, real estate agents, and the Lewis Grocery in the two-story building on the corner. If you go into the alley behind the buildings, you can easily distinguish between the individual structures.

Turn right onto Third Street and walk one block to First Avenue North. For a better view, cross to the north side of the road and go right. Look south across the street to the set of balconies at 256–260 First Avenue North. This is the Binnie/Bishop Hotel.

4 Binnie/Bishop Hotel
256–260 1st Ave. N

The original portion of this old hotel was constructed in 1912 by pioneer blacksmith Henry Binnie. When the hitching posts were removed in front of the nearby grocery in 1914, Binnie foresaw the end of the blacksmith trade and decided to enlarge the hotel. The original, western portion was two stories, while the 1921 addition is three stories, so a balcony and a common roofline were added to unify the front. (Look for the staircase on the balcony that connects the floors.) The elaborate grape details of the ironwork were added in 1948 by owner Roy Bishop. Look for the stamp of the Chattanooga Roof and Foundry on the iron pilasters! The building is a local historic landmark.

ST. PETERSBURG MUSEUM OF HISTORY

5 Tamiami Hotel
242 1st Ave. N

Next door to the Binne/Bishop Hotel stands the Mediterranean Revival–style Tamiami Hotel, constructed in 1924 by the Schooley-Murphy Company. The word "Tamiami" is a blend of Tampa and Miami, and was given to the highway connecting those two cities around 1915.

ST. PETERSBURG MUSEUM OF HISTORY

Continuing to the end of the block, you'll pass a long two-story building with a brick trim inlay. This is Peacock Row.

6 Peacock Row
208–226 1st Ave. N

The masonry vernacular building known as Peacock Row was constructed in 1920 to offer an additional 49 hotel rooms for guests of the Detroit Hotel. Its ground floor housed early commercial occupants like the Tourist Cafe, the Palm Book Store, Campbell & Mixon Fruits, and George Atherton's Confections. The name "Peacock Row" was often used to describe a place where the wealthy and well-preened would show themselves off; it was probably affixed to this building aspirationally.

CITY OF ST. PETERSBURG

When you reach Second Street, go south and walk back to Central Avenue. Head west again on Central to the corner of Fourth Street. On the southeast corner is the Empire Building.

7 Empire Building
300 Central Ave.

ST. PETERSBURG MUSEUM OF HISTORY

Early merchant J. Bruce Smith dubbed this "the busy corner" and built this high-rise in 1925 to house his clothing store. It was designed by M. Leo Elliott, a prominent architect who designed many buildings in Tampa and Sarasota. It was renamed the Empire Building in 1933, perhaps in a nod to the famous skyscraper in New York, which opened in 1931. During World War II, the building was used as the headquarters of the Army Air Forces Basic Training Center, No. 6. In 1963, it was expanded upward by three floors and the exterior was altered significantly. At that time it was renamed the Coronet Apartments.

8 Municipal Services Center/ First Federal Bank
1 4th St. N

TAMPA-HILLSBOROUGH COUNTY PUBLIC LIBRARY SYSTEM

Today's Municipal Services Center hides a surprise. Underneath exterior panels of a "fractured glass aggregate" lie the remains of a lovely 1926 Gothic-style building of limestone, brick, and terra cotta. A 1958 addition expanded the 10-story First Federal Building eastward and covered the older structure and its new addition in a skin of enameled tiles. The City of St. Petersburg bought the building in 1994 and converted it into the Municipal Services Center.

On the northwest corner of Fourth Street and Central Avenue is the Snell Building and Arcade.

9 Snell Building and Arcade
405 Central Ave.

In 1908, the northwest corner of Fourth Street and Central Avenue was bought by real estate agent Noel Mitchell, who made it famous as "Mitchell's Corner." Later developer Perry Snell broke ground on the stunning Snell Building and Arcade in 1928. Designed by architects Kiehnel and Elliott, it is made of glazed terra cotta on the upper floors and Florida keystone and Georgia marble on the ground floor, which featured 24 stores in its arcade. It later became a Walgreen Drugs and then Rutland's Department Store. In the 1980s, the building was restored and added to the National and Local Registers of Historic Places. In the early 2000s, the upper floors became condominiums. If the arcade is open, walk through!

TAMPA-HILLSBOROUGH COUNTY PUBLIC LIBRARY SYSTEM

Cross Fourth Street and continue west along Central Avenue. Midblock, at 437 Central Avenue, you'll pass McCrory's.

10 McCrory's
441 Central Ave.

Built in 1904, this building is remembered as the McCrory five-and-dime, which opened here in 1912. The building underwent a significant renovation in the late 1920s to present the streamlined appearance you see today. A 40-room hotel occupied the upper floors (you can still see the ghost sign of the Hotel Alden when you view the build-

ing from the east). McCrory's closed in 1999 but the marquee sign from 1939 remains and is listed on the city's registry of historic signs.

DID YOU KNOW?

In 1908, Noel Mitchell placed benches in front of his real estate office for his patrons. They were popular, and neighboring businesses followed suit, until there were thousands of benches lining city streets. A 1916 ordinance mandated that the benches be painted green, and they became famous, appearing on thousands of postcards and magazines. While they were viewed as a symbol of hospitality by the White community, Black residents were not permitted to sit on the green benches, and they are often remembered as a symbol of division.

Continuing west on Central Avenue, you'll pass the Florida Arcade at 449 Central. On the northeast corner of Central Avenue and Fifth Street is the Kress Building.

11 Kress Building
475 Central Ave.

Built in 1927, this lovely building housed the Kress five-and-dime store. Kress buildings throughout the county often share common details like the yellow terra-cotta tile that covers the building and the parapet at the top, which still features the name Kress. The store closed in 1981. Like the adjacent McCrory's, it offered a popular lunch counter, the site of sit-ins during the civil rights movement. It is a local historic landmark.

Cross Fifth Street and continue on Central Avenue, passing the old Rutland Department Store (now Florida CraftArt). Midblock you'll find the four-story Alexander Hotel.

12 Alexander Hotel
535 Central Ave.

This striking Neoclassical-style building was built in 1919 for wealthy North Carolina lumberman Jacob Alexander. Designed by architect Neel Reid, the hotel's formal Palladian entryway, symmetrical facade, and three-tiered veranda with Tuscan columns make it one of the most attractive buildings in the city. It was renovated and designated a local historic landmark in 1986.

On the south side of the street is St. Petersburg Federal Savings and Loan Association.

13 St. Petersburg Federal Savings and Loan Association
556 Central Ave.

This 1941 Art Deco structure was built for the St. Petersburg Federal Savings and Loan Association. The second largest of the city's five S&Ls, it was

unique as it was founded in 1935 by three women: sisters Cornelia, Elsie, and Ilona Somp. It was designated a local historic landmark in 1999.

Cross Sixth Street onto the 600 Block of Central Avenue. Midway on the north side of the block is the Crislip Arcade.

14 Crislip Arcade

645 and 689 Central Ave.

Most buildings on the 600 Block were constructed during the 1920s' boom and then entered a period of decline beginning in the 1960s. Much of the north side of the block, including the striking Crislip Arcade, built in 1925, faced the threat of demolition in 2006 but was saved by a compromise between artists, preservationists, and the developer who owned the buildings. Today, the arcade is the centerpiece of one of the liveliest blocks in the city, with hip boutiques, restaurants, and a nightclub.

Just west of the Crislip Arcade, you'll come to the ornate marquee of the Floridian Social Club. This was the Alexander National Bank/ State Theater.

15 Alexander National Bank/ State Theater

687 Central Ave.

Built in 1924 as the Alexander National Bank, this large Beaux Arts–style building was designed by prominent Atlanta architect Neel Reid, who also designed the nearby Alexander Hotel. The bank closed following the stock market crash of 1929. In 1950, it opened as the State Theatre with a floating movie screen. The theater closed in the 1980s and reopened as a popular live music venue from 1991

until 2017. A real estate broker renovated it into a luxury nightclub, partially out of nostalgia—his parents had their first date there when it was a movie theater. It is a local historic landmark.

Make sure to also see the Green-Richman Arcade at 689 Central Avenue, another local historic landmark built in 1926.

DID YOU KNOW?

In the mid-1920s, there were a dozen shopping arcades in St. Petersburg, a passage through a building with small shops on both sides. They offered protection from the sunshine and downpours of summer and created a shortcut between blocks. Arcades enjoyed a heyday then fell out of favor. Today, there are four remaining arcades that are again appreciated for their utility and uniqueness.

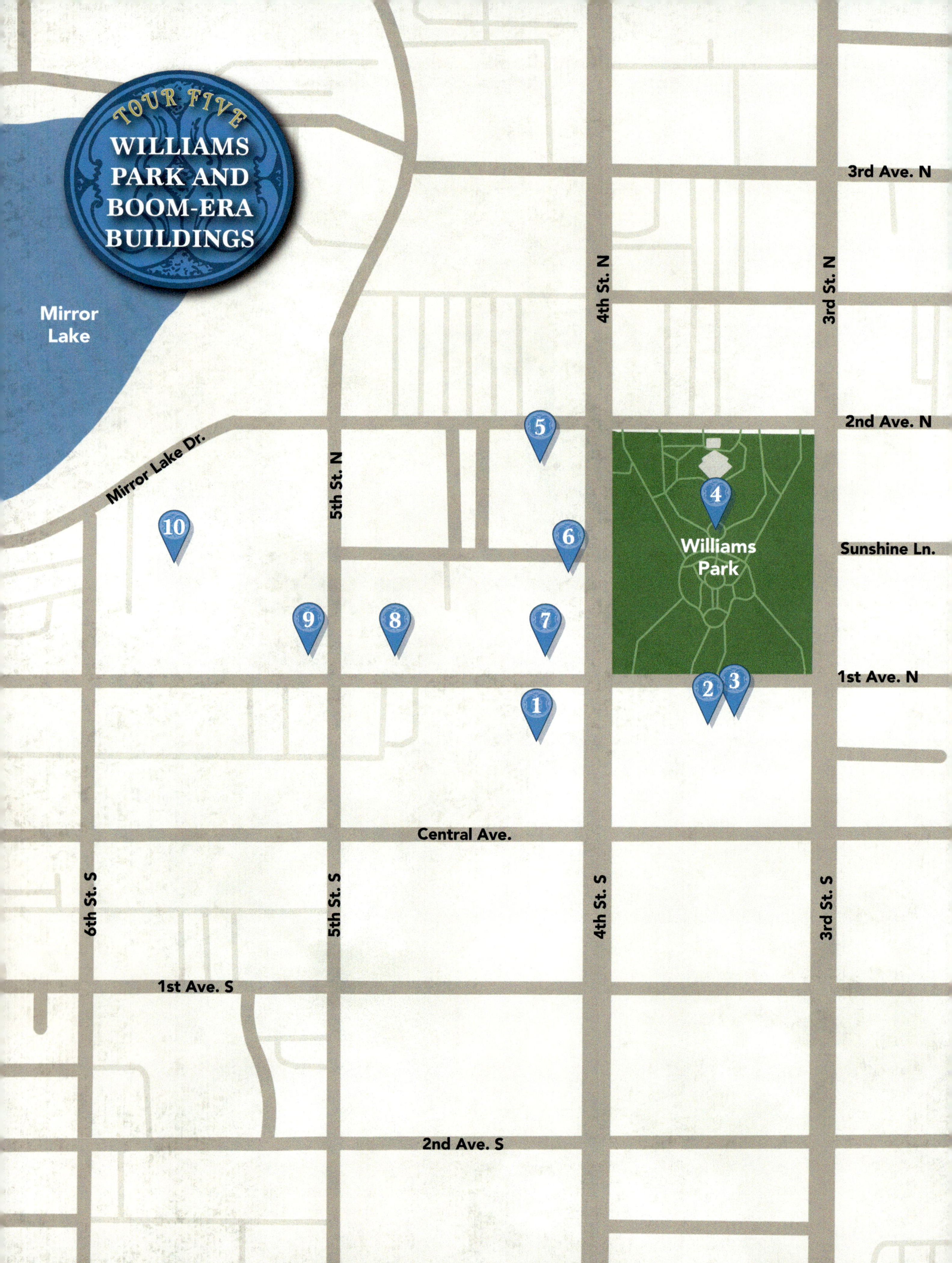

TOUR FIVE
WILLIAMS PARK AND BOOM-ERA BUILDINGS
Mirror Lake
Mirror Lake Dr.
3rd Ave. N
2nd Ave. N
Sunshine Ln.
1st Ave. N
Central Ave.
1st Ave. S
2nd Ave. S
6th St. S
5th St. N
5th St. S
4th St. N
4th St. S
3rd St. N
3rd St. S
Williams Park
1
2
3
4
5
6
7
8
9
10

TOUR FIVE

WILLIAMS PARK AND BOOM-ERA BUILDINGS

Approximately 0.6 miles

This tour begins at one of the city's most photographed buildings and ends at an award-winning mid-century modern courthouse.

Begin at the southwest corner of Fourth Street and First Avenue North.

1 Open Air Post Office

74 4th St. N

TAMPA-HILLSBOROUGH COUNTY PUBLIC LIBRARY SYSTEM

The 1916 Open Air Post Office was envisioned by postmaster Roy S. Hanna, who proposed a building open on three sides that highlighted the city's idyllic weather. Architect George W. Stewart modeled the post office after the Ospedale Degli Innocenti, a children's hospital in Florence, Italy. The building is listed on the National and the Local Registers of Historic Places.

Make your way to the northeast corner of Fourth Street and First Avenue North. Follow the sidewalk east along First Avenue North and look toward the south side of the street. Midblock is the Women's Town Improvement Association.

2 Women's Town Improvement Association

336 1st Ave. N

Built in 1913, this attractive two-story Neoclassical structure was the headquarters for the Women's Town Improvement Association, a group of well-connected, ambitious women responsible for many early civic improvements. (The club was not open to women of color, who created their own service clubs.) During the 1920s, this building was used by both the YWCA and the Board of Trade, which focused on increasing tourism to the city; in that role it housed the city's first public restroom! The building was altered in 1931, creating the Art Deco, cast-stone facade seen on the first floor today. It is a local historic landmark.

CITY OF ST. PETERSBURG

The eight-story hotel next door was built as the Dennis Hotel.

3 Dennis Hotel

326 1st Ave. N

CITY OF ST. PETERSBURG

This Beaux Arts–style hotel was designed by Harry F. Cunningham, a prominent national architect who also designed the St. Petersburg Shuffleboard Club, and the Nebraska State Capitol. It was built by Greek immigrant Nick Dennis, who learned the hospitality trade at esteemed establishments like Delmonico's in New York and the Willard Hotel in Washington, DC.

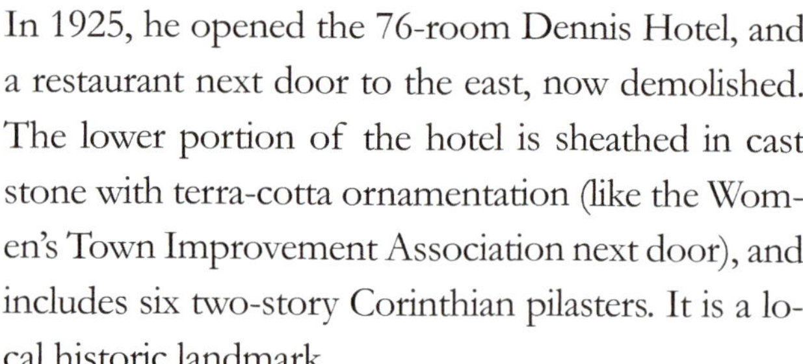

In 1925, he opened the 76-room Dennis Hotel, and a restaurant next door to the east, now demolished. The lower portion of the hotel is sheathed in cast stone with terra-cotta ornamentation (like the Women's Town Improvement Association next door), and includes six two-story Corinthian pilasters. It is a local historic landmark.

Now enter Williams Park near the Veterans Memorial.

4 Williams Park
Between Third and Fourth Streets North and First and Second Avenues North

Originally called City Park and later renamed for city cofounder John Williams, this was the first park in St. Petersburg. For decades it hosted regular band concerts, shuffleboard games, horseshoes, and card parties. Walk through to see the bandstand, a feature of the park since 1895. This 1954 iteration was designed by architect William B. Harvard and has won numerous architectural awards. The park also features a number of monuments including a veterans memorial (made up of columns from the American Bank and Trust Building on Central Avenue, which was demolished in the 1970s despite public outcry) and a sculpture of Revolutionary War hero Thaddeus Kościuszko.

TAMPA-HILLSBOROUGH COUNTY PUBLIC LIBRARY SYSTEM

At the northwest corner of the park at Third Street and Second Avenue North, cross Fourth Street to view the Cathedral of St. Peter.

5 The Cathedral of St. Peter
140 4th St. N

One of the oldest churches in the city, St. Peter's Episcopal Cathedral was consecrated in 1899 on land donated by early philanthropist Edwin Tomlinson and was expanded in 1926. The church inadvertently foiled a campaign speech by Ronald Reagan in 1980 in nearby Williams Park that coincided with a funeral. The church's tradition was to ring the bell once for every year of the deceased person's life. Reagan's aides were apoplectic when they learned the age of the recently departed: 94 years old! The church is a local historic landmark.

TAMPA-HILLSBOROUGH COUNTY PUBLIC LIBRARY SYSTEM

Return south on Fourth Street. Midblock you will encounter the facade of the First Baptist Church.

6 First Baptist Church
120 4th St. N

Prominent local architect George Feltham designed this church in 1922. It is Neoclassical, with an imposing Greek Temple form, made up of polished beige brick and yellow stained glass windows. In a creative solution to a fierce debate over the proposed demolition of this local historic landmark, the back portion of the church was demolished in 2008 while the facade was preserved and a parking garage built behind it.

MONICA KILE

Continue south on Fourth Street, then go right on First Avenue North to the Princess Martha Hotel.

7 Princess Martha Hotel

411 1st Ave. N

Opened as the Mason Hotel in January of 1924, this was one of the 10 boom-era hotels. It was later sold and renamed the Princess Martha, after the wife of a major investor. Look for a large M over the door, as well as garlands in the shape of the letter M near the top of the building, which originally stood for Mason but also worked for Martha! The hotel helped lure the New York Yankees here for spring training in 1925: players stayed here on the American Plan (meals included) for $8 a man, two men to a room. Like the nearby Snell Arcade, this building has a full basement that runs under the sidewalks. It is now a senior living facility and a local historic landmark.

Continue west on First Avenue North. On the corner of Fifth Street is the Christ United Methodist Church.

8 Christ United Methodist Church

467 1st Ave. N

The congregation of this church dates back to 1892. This is their third church built on this site since 1906. This 1953 structure was designed by local architect Archie Parish and increased the church's seats from 1,000 to more than 1,700, a sign of the tremendous population boom of the 1950s. Make sure to look up from the sidewalk to see the unique heads along the windows, and note the Florida keystone coral on the first floor.

Continue west. At the northwest corner of First Avenue North and Fifth Street is the Suwannee Hotel.

9 Suwannee Hotel

501 1st Ave. N

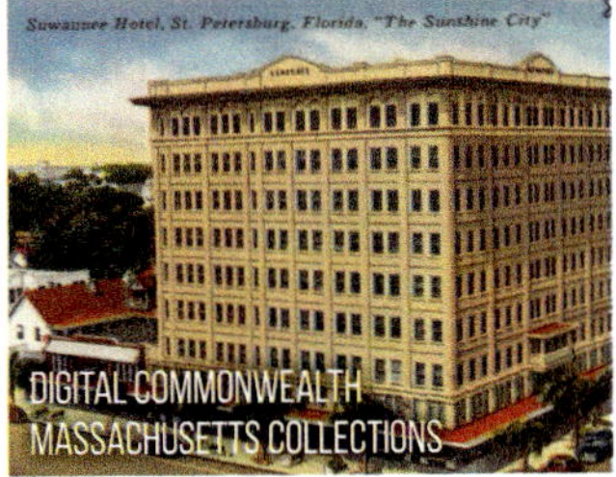

When it opened in 1923, the 118-room Suwannee Hotel boasted "running ice water" in every room, along with an electric "taxi fan," which would run for one hour when a nickel was inserted in the slot. It was built by John Brown, a banker who also served as the county clerk. Comedian Buster Keaton stayed here in 1933, and during World War II it was the only major hotel in the city that didn't house military trainees. Converted to offices in the 1980s, it has been owned by Pinellas County government since the early 2000s.

Continue on First Avenue North. Before Sixth Street, take the steps up to the mezzanine of the Judicial Building.

10 St. Petersburg Judicial Building

545 1st Ave. N

Built in 1968 by award-winning local architect Glenn Johnson, this Brutalist-style courthouse was the architect's favorite of all his buildings. The building's robust form is meant to project strength and solidarity, fitting for a courthouse.

The tour ends here. If you exit down the stairs on the north end, you can take the Marvelous Mirror Lake Tour.

TOUR SIX
MARVELOUS MIRROR LAKE
6th Ave. N
Earle Ave.
7th St. N
6th St. N
5th St. N
Dartmoor St. N
5th Ave. N
4th Ave. N
4th Ave. N
5th St. N
Mirror Lake Dr. N
3rd Ave. N
8th St. N
Mirror Lake
2nd Ave. N
2nd Ave. N
Mirror Lake Dr. N
Arlington Ave. N
1st Ave. N
8th St. S
7th St. S
6th St. S
5th St. S
Central Ave.
1
2
3
4
5
6
7
8
9
10
11
12
13
14
15

TOUR SIX
MARVELOUS MIRROR LAKE
Approximately 0.7 miles

Originally known as Reservoir Lake, this was the original source of drinking water for the city, and an early civic center, with the city's first schools, many early churches, a recreational complex, and City Hall. The perimeter of the lake is city-owned parkland.

Start this tour in front of City Hall.

1 City Hall
175 5th St. N

One of a handful of buildings constructed during the Great Depression, City Hall was built with a New Deal grant from the Public Works Administration in 1937. It is considered to be Art Moderne in style, with Mediterranean Revival and Art Deco influences. Two paintings by artist George Snow Hill once hung on either side of the split interior staircase. One of the murals was long decried as racially insensitive and in 1966 was torn from the wall in a protest that helped spark civil rights activities in the city. That space remains empty today. Visitors may enter this local historic landmark during business hours.

CITY OF ST. PETERSBURG

Walk east on Second Avenue North. Note the bricks that pave the alley behind City Hall. A careful eye can see the fingerprints of the workers who handled the bricks. Behind City Hall is the Domestic Science and Manual Training School/City Hall Annex.

2 Domestic Science and Manual Training School/ City Hall Annex
440 2nd Ave. N

CITY OF ST. PETERSBURG

Don't miss this charming brick building (one of the first to be built in the city using that material) tucked behind City Hall. In 1901, local philanthropist Edwin Tomlinson donated the land for this building, which was used for classes in manual training, physical culture, and military science. Tomlinson was a generous philanthropist, funding many educational opportunities and events in the city. The building is a local historic landmark.

Retrace your steps to Fifth Street and look at the public art featuring red chairs across the street from City Hall. This is the *Face the Jury* Sculpture.

3 *Face the Jury* Sculpture
South corner of Mirror Lake Dr. and 5th St.

This publicly funded art installation was created in 2006 by artist Douglas Kornfeld. The 12 chairs

MONICA KILE

facing east are meant to represent a jury, while the single chair on the corner facing southwest represents a person on trial. It was inspired by the artist's own experience serving on a jury; each chair was modeled after a juror with whom he served. The chairs are divided into groups of seven and five, the same way his jury split. It sits behind the St. Petersburg Judicial Building.

Go north on Fifth Street. As the street bends slightly right, you'll pass a three-story apartment structure in yellow brick. These are the Poulson Apartments.

4 Poulson Apartments
215–217 5th St. N

The 1921 Poulson Apartments are an excellent example of the winter tourist apartment houses that were built throughout St. Petersburg in the first few decades of the 1900s. Eventually demand outstripped the available apartments, and large hotels were built to accommodate the increasing tourist population during the 1920s' boom. There are a dwindling number of tourist apartment houses remaining in the city as development pressures lead to their demolition.

MONICA KILE

Continue north on Fifth Street. As you approach Third Avenue North, you will see the Mirror Lake Library.

5 Mirror Lake Library
280 5th St. N

Constructed in 1916, the Beaux Arts–style Mirror Lake Library was the first public library in St. Petersburg. It was funded by a grant from the Andrew Carnegie Foundation. The largely self-educated Carnegie believed that libraries were a great way to help the "deserving poor" and funded more than 2,500 public libraries throughout the English-speaking world. The library is a local historic landmark.

MONICA KILE

Turn left on Mirror Lake Drive and cross to the north side of the street. Walk about a block to the Shuffleboard Club.

6 Shuffleboard Club
559 Mirror Lake Dr. N

For over 100 years, the Shuffleboard Club has epitomized the leisurely life of the Sunshine City. The first two courts were built in 1923; the following year several players formed the Mirror Lake Park Shuffleboard Club, the first of its kind in the world. Construction on the clubhouse began in 1927, a space for bridge and dancing was added in 1937, and the grandstands were built in 1939. The official rules of shuffleboard were written here, and the center line of the shuffleboard court is nicknamed Central Avenue, for St. Petersburg's main street.

TAMPA-HILLSBOROUGH COUNTY PUBLIC LIBRARY SYSTEM

In the early 2000s the Club attracted renewed interest, in part by hosting Friday night games with music and food. Today, membership again approaches 3,000 members, and the club is celebrated in national media. It sits on city-owned land and is a local historic landmark.

Explore inside the grounds, where you'll also find the location of the St. Petersburg Chess Club (or Chess Divan, as it was called in the 1930s), and the St. Petersburg Lawn Bowling Club.

7 St. Petersburg Lawn Bowling Club

Inside the grounds of the Shuffleboard Club

TAMPA-HILLSBOROUGH COUNTY PUBLIC LIBRARY SYSTEM

The city's first lawn bowling courts were constructed here in 1917. When the inaugural match was played in February, organizers boasted that it was the first time the popular Scotch and Canadian game had been played in Florida and maybe even the entire South. The first permanent clubhouse structure was built in 1918. It is listed on the National Register of Historic Places and is a designated local historic landmark.

Walk to the back of the complex and look across Fourth Avenue North to the Coliseum. Walk through the gate to look back at what were originally the front doors of the Chess and Lawn Bowling Clubs. When Fourth Avenue North was made one-way as part of the off-ramp of the interstate, it severed what was once a pedestrian-friendly connection between these two recreation centers.

8 The Coliseum

535 4th Ave. N

The Coliseum was built in 1924 to provide entertainment to a growing tourist population. It soon became a major destination for performers of the swing era, and its 13,000-square-foot white maple dance floor became a popular dancing venue. Its large arched roof is supported by 13 wooden trusses, and the ceiling is made of tongue-and-groove wooden boards. Entertainers who performed here included Duke Ellington, Louis Armstrong, Count Basie, and Glenn Miller. During the 1930s, a hurricane damaged the structure, forcing the removal of two Moorish-inspired towers. The ballroom dance scene from the 1985 movie *Cocoon* was filmed here. The building was purchased by the city in 1989 and designated a local historic landmark in 1994.

TAMPA-HILLSBOROUGH COUNTY PUBLIC LIBRARY SYSTEM

Exit the Shuffleboard Club, back to Mirror Lake Drive. The tour heads counterclockwise around the western part of the lake. After crossing Seventh Street, you will see the St. Petersburg High School/Mirror Lake Condominiums.

9 St. Petersburg High School/ Mirror Lake Condominiums

701 Mirror Lake Dr.

There have been five different schools on the shores of Mirror Lake over the years. Remarkably, three are still standing, the most prominent being this high school building, constructed in 1919. It was designed by William Ittner, the most prolific school architect in the United States. In just a few years, the city's population outgrew this building and a new high school was built

MONICA KILE

outside of downtown in 1926. This building became a middle school for girls, and in 1991 was converted to a private condominium. It is a designated local historic landmark.

Continuing around the lake, at the corner of Grove Street is the Mirror Lake Christian Church.

10 Mirror Lake Christian Chuch

737 3rd Ave. N

Built in 1926, this Mediterranean Revival–style building with Mission-style influences was one of the most impressive churches built during the boom. Its interior features are equally as stunning, with floors of hardwood and terrazzo, ornamental plaster moldings, and stained glass windows. Its sanctuary seated 1,000 congregants. Declining membership led to its closure and sale in 1992, and it became a private event space. Today it once again serves as a church. The neighborhood behind the church has an interesting collection of tourist apartments and small homes from the 1910s and 1920s.

MONICA KILE

At the corner of Third Avenue North and Mirror Lake Drive is St. Petersburg Junior High School/Tomlinson Center.

11 St. Petersburg Junior High School/Tomlinson Center

296 Mirror Lake Dr. N

Opened in 1924 as a coed junior high school, this building was also designed by William Ittner. It became an all-boys school after the former high school was converted to an all-girls junior high. It later became a vocational training school, and then the Tomlinson Adult Education Center. It closed in 2021. Note the impressive owls, which signify wisdom, above the doorway.

MONICA KILE

Continue along Mirror Lake Drive, now heading south. On the right you will see the Cade Allen House.

12 Cade Allen House

250 Mirror Lake Dr. N

Built in 1936 as a private residence for Mrs. Ena S. Jackson, this home was referred to by the *St. Petersburg Times* as "one of the most beautiful and luxurious in the city" in 1937. It was built by local contractor Cade Allen who became famous for the use of stone veneers on his buildings. Limited by Florida's dearth of natural stone (though he did use some of the native coquina), he shipped in stone from throughout the Southeast. This building is now used as an office. The former home immediately to the south is also by Cade Allen, featuring his signature stonework around the front door.

MONICA KILE

Continue along Mirror Lake Drive to where it meets Arlington Avenue. Here is the Unitarian Universalist Church.

13 Unitarian Universalist Church
100 Mirror Lake Dr. N

MONICA KILE

This church was built in 1929 by two local congregations, the Universalists and the Unitarians, who joined forces in 1925, some 36 years before the two congregations combined nationally. The building was designed by an architect from Boston who had to be persuaded by congregants that, despite media coverage to the contrary, it did get cold enough in St. Petersburg that the church would need heating. Alternately described as Mission Revival, Mediterranean Revival, or Spanish Revival, it blends elements of each style. Hand-crafted Spanish tiles on the roof were surplus material from the construction of the Don Cesar Hotel at St. Pete Beach, donated by the contractor who constructed both buildings.

Turn right on Arlington Avenue, which was home to St. Petersburg's first two synagogues as well as to many of the homes and businesses of the city's early Jewish community. On the right just behind the church property is the Elks Lodge.

14 Elks Lodge
735 Arlington Ave. N

MONICA KILE

Constructed in 1924, this building served for decades as the Elks Lodge and Club. For a time in the early 1930s, it provided offices to the Central Casting Bureau as they sought talent for *Playthings of Desire*, a movie filmed here during St. Petersburg's brief stint as the Hollywood of Florida. Artist Mark Dixon Dodd also hosted his School of Art here in 1933.

A little farther up the block on the right is a building with a tile roof. This was the Temple Beth-El.

15 Temple Beth-El
757 Arlington Ave. N

This building was constructed in 1933 as the first synagogue of Temple Beth-El, the first Reform Jewish congregation in St. Petersburg. The congregation formally organized in 1928, making it the second synagogue founded in the city, after B'nai Israel (which started in 1923). By 1961, the congregation had outgrown this structure and moved across town. The first synagogue constructed by Congregation B'nai Israel was located farther west on Arlington Avenue but has since been demolished.

MONICA KILE

The tour concludes here. You're just a stone's throw from Central Avenue and lots of great dining options.

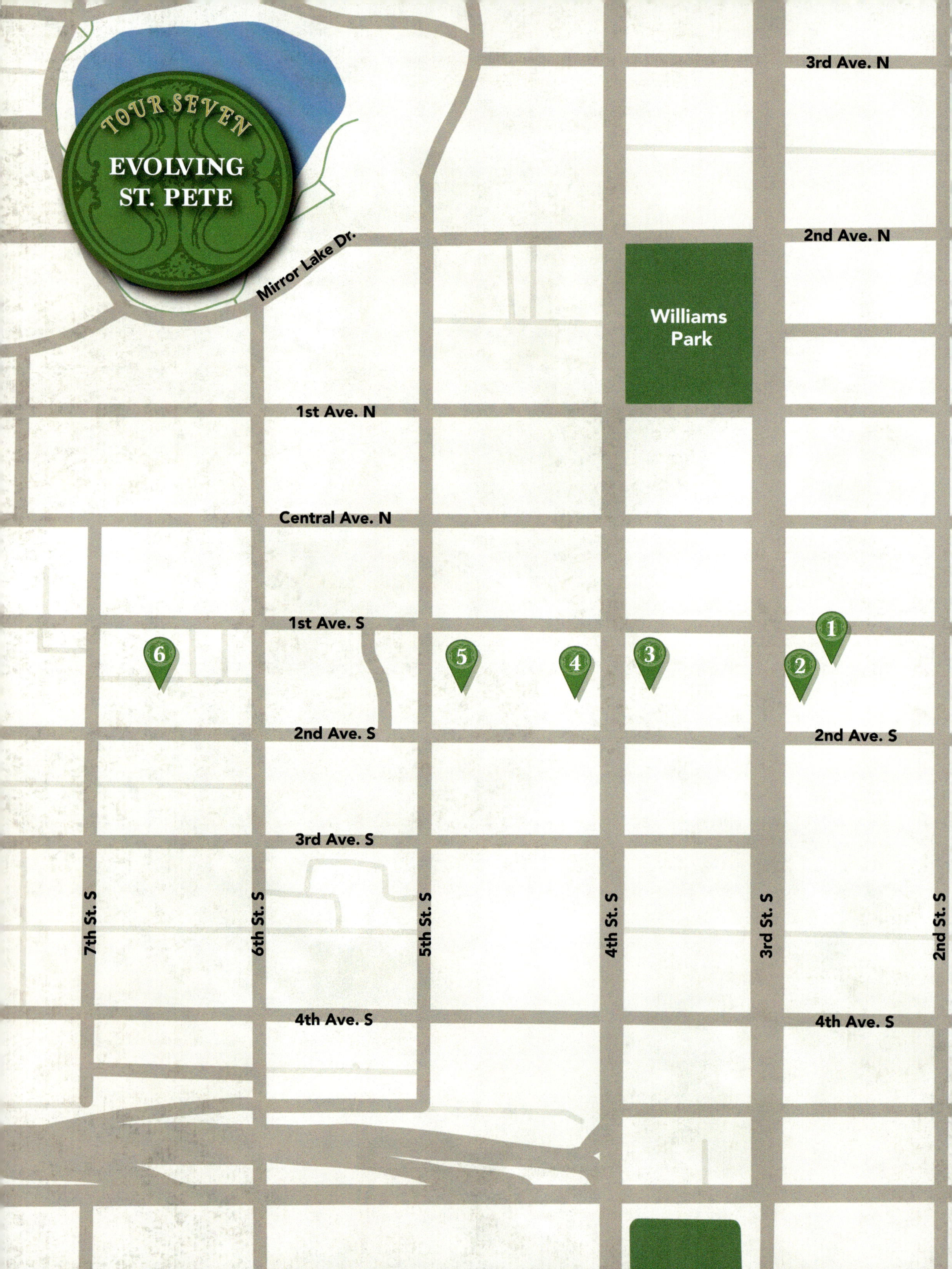
TOUR SEVEN
EVOLVING ST. PETE
3rd Ave. N
2nd Ave. N
Mirror Lake Dr.
Williams Park
1st Ave. N
Central Ave. N
1st Ave. S
1
2
3
4
5
6
2nd Ave. S
2nd Ave. S
3rd Ave. S
7th St. S
6th St. S
5th St. S
4th St. S
3rd St. S
2nd St. S
4th Ave. S
4th Ave. S

TOUR SEVEN

EVOLVING ST. PETE

Approximately 0.4 miles

This tour highlights successful examples of the adaptive reuse of historic buildings. Many of these early buildings were positioned to take advantage of the railroad line, which ran down today's First Avenue South and helped create the city's early infrastructure. Others highlight the city's early social history.

Start this tour on the southeast corner of First Avenue South and Third Street South. The brick building with arched windows and doors on the south side of First Avenue South is the St. Petersburg Hardware Building.

1 St. Petersburg Hardware Building

260 1st Ave. S

CITY OF ST. PETERSBURG

This 1911 building was originally the warehouse of a large hardware and furnishings store, St. Petersburg Hardware, whose location provided easy access for freight deliveries from the railroad. A small, wood-frame structure abutted this building to the west (where the landscaped courtyard is located today); that building housed the *St. Petersburg Times* printing press from 1912 to 1921. Later the wood-frame building became the Stag Hotel "for older men" and was torn down when the hardware building was rehabilitated in 1983, a time when the future of downtown was uncertain. The rehabilitation brought out the charm of the historic building, leaving bricks, joists, and beams exposed, and changed the original loading bays on First Avenue South into arched doorways and windows.

Go south on Third Street. Just before you reach Second Avenue South, you will see another brick building on the east side of Third Street South. This was the first fire station.

2 The First Fire Station

128 3rd St. S

This 1911 brick vernacular building was the city's first fire station. It provided accommodation not just for firemen, but also for the horses whose job it was to pull the steam engine! You can still see the bays where the fire wagons, and later trucks, were stored. Following the death of the first fire chief in 1912, a new chief, J.T. McNulty, was appointed and served for the next 24 years. It is after him that the adjacent buildings, McNulty Lofts and McNulty Station, took their name.

MONICA KILE

Retrace your steps north on Third Street to First Avenue South. Head west on First Avenue South, just like an Orange Belt passenger train would have done when leaving the city. Turn left to head south on Fourth Street South. Midblock, on your left, you will come upon the Masonic Lodge.

MONICA KILE

3 Masonic Lodge
114 4th St. S

This 1955 building replaced an earlier 1916 structure on this same site. The St. Petersburg Freemasons Lodge 139 was the second Masonic lodge founded in the city (after the African American Masonic Lodge 109 in the Gas Plant neighborhood). When this building was constructed, a time capsule was placed in the cornerstone, including copies of the two daily newspapers, membership rosters, and a letter from the oldest living member of the lodge. The distinctive marble on the facade and the cantilevered concrete awning, as well as the clean geometric lines, are hallmarks of mid-century modern design.

Across Fourth Street from the Masonic Lodge, at the corner of Second Avenue South and Fourth Street, you'll get a good view of the Tramor Cafeteria.

4 Tramor Cafeteria
123 4th St. S

This building was constructed in 1929 as Bob's Cafeteria, and in 1939 became the Tramor Cafeteria, named after a hotel in Atlantic City, New Jersey (see page 13 for info on cafeterias). The name also had a subliminal message—implying that, as a Tramor customer, you could get "more on your tray." Visitors get a hint of the Mediterranean influences from the outside, but the building is even more glorious inside, designed to make guests feel like they are in the courtyard of a Spanish hacienda, looking up toward a blue, clouded sky and surrounded by twisting concrete columns and barrel tiles. The Tramor was used to feed soldiers training in St. Petersburg during World War II and later was purchased by the adjacent *St. Petersburg Times* as a cafeteria for its staff. It is a local historic landmark.

LIBRARY OF CONGRESS

Walk south to Second Avenue South. If you haven't already crossed Fourth Street South, do so now. Head west on Second Avenue South for one block. On the northeast corner of Fifth Street and Second Avenue South is the historic YMCA.

5 The Historic YMCA
116 5th St. S

MONICA KILE

This handsome Mediterranean Revival–style building held its grand opening on June 20, 1927, as the local YMCA. It included a gymnasium, a swimming pool, locker rooms, a dormitory, a cafeteria, showers, and a running track. Its dormitory provided accommodation to young men new to town, and during World War II it hosted thousands of servicemen. Like all of early St. Petersburg, the YMCA did not welcome all citizens equally; the grand downtown building was off-limits to Black members. (After prodding from the community, the Colored Branch YMCA opened in 1945, later renamed the Melrose Park YMCA). The YMCA sold this building in 2001 and it remains empty. It is listed on the Local Register of Historic Places.

From the southeast corner of Second Avenue South and Fifth Street, you can get an interesting perspective on the evolution of housing in St. Pete. See *Did You Know?* on this page.

Continue west on Second Avenue South for 1.5 blocks. On the right is the stately Endicott Funeral Home.

6 Endicott Funeral Home

655 2nd Ave. S

This structure was built in 1924 as the Endicott Funeral Home (later the Palms Memorial Funeral Home), touted for its sun parlor, the stateliness of its rooms, and the professionalism of its staff. James Endicott was the president of the Florida Funeral Directors and Embalmers Association. An affluent man, his home is still standing near Williams Park (page 12.) The building is now home to a popular steak house.

STATE ARCHIVES OF FLORIDA

MONICA KILE

DID YOU KNOW?

Since the city first began to draw tourists in large numbers in the 1910s, there has been an evolution in both short- and long-term housing in St. Petersburg. On the southwest corner of Second Avenue South and Fifth Street, you can see a three-story tourist apartment built in 1915 as the Winchell Apartments. Beyond it to the west you can see a 14-story high-rise; to the northwest there is a similar 16-story building. These were both built as federally subsidized housing for elderly people in the late 1960s. Eight other similar buildings were built downtown between the late 1960s and the early 1980s in an attempt to revive a moribund downtown with new residents. They may have had the opposite effect, contributing instead to the city's reputation as the "world's largest above-ground cemetery." Finally, on the southeast corner, you'll see a modern-day apartment building catering to both year-round working residents as well as visitors who may only use their apartment in the winter season.

TOUR EIGHT
THE DYNAMIC DEUCES
6th Ave. S
22nd St. S
Fairfield Ave. S
I-275
I-275
7th Ave. S
7th Ave. S
8th Ave. S
I-275
I-275
9th Ave. S
9th Ave. S
Irving Ave. S
Jordan Park St.
Union St.
21st St. S
20th St. S
10th Ave. S
11th Ave. S
24th St. S
11th Ave. S
22nd Ln. S
12th Ave. S
12th Ave. S
25th St. S
22nd St. S
13th Ave. S
13th Ave. S
13th Ave. S
Melrose Ave. S
Melrose Ave. S
14th Ave. S
14th Ave. S
14th Ave. S
15th Ave. S
15th Ave. S
1
2
3
4
5
6
7
8
9

TOUR EIGHT

THE DYNAMIC DEUCES

Approximately 0.9 miles

The area known as the Deuces (for the 2s in the name of 22nd Street) is a historically African American main street that began to develop in the 1920s. By 1960 there were 111 businesses here, three-quarters of them Black-owned.

You'll start this tour at the historic Manhattan Casino building before walking underneath the interstate, which sliced through the neighborhood in the early 1980s causing massive disruption. Along the way, be sure to take in the excellent African American Heritage Trail signs.

1 Manhattan Casino/ Sno Peak Drive-In

642 22nd St. S

Built in 1925 as the Jordan Dance Hall, this later became the Manhattan Casino. It was said to have the best hard oak dance floor in the state and was the site of community events like proms and coronations. Famous entertainers like Count Basie, Duke Ellington, Ella Fitzgerald, Ray Charles, Mahalia Jackson, Louis Armstrong, Ike and Tina Turner, and Sam Cooke performed here. The ballroom closed in 1968 and was later purchased by the city and designated a local historic landmark.

Across the street was a drive-in restaurant called the Sno Peak. People who couldn't get in the Manhattan Casino would visit for a burger and listen to the music from the windows instead. Stokely Carmichael spoke in the Sno Peak parking lot in 1967.

CITY OF ST. PETERSBURG

Just south of the Manhattan Casino is the Elder Jordan Sr. Sculpture.

2 Elder Jordan Sr. Sculpture

CITY OF ST. PETERSBURG

This sculpture depicts legendary city leader and developer Elder Jordan Sr. Jordan moved to St. Pete in 1904, where he became a successful entrepreneur, eventually owning significant amounts of real estate. A major advocate for education, the city's second African American elementary school was named after him, as was the Jordan Park Housing Complex, for which he donated land.

Continue south on 22nd Street, passing under the interstate. At the southwest corner of 22nd Street and Ninth Avenue South is Harden's Grocery.

3 Harden's Grocery

901 22nd St. S

Businessman George Washington constructed this building in 1939 and leased it to grocer Sidney Harden in 1942. At that time, there were approximately 125 small, independent groceries in St. Petersburg, of which 11 were owned by African Americans. Harden's Grocery sold popular items like hog heads, possums, raccoons, chitterlings, go-

pher turtles, raw peanuts, snuff, and kerosene. When local residents were struggling, Harden would allow purchases on credit or give them work. The store closed in 1992 and has since been home to several restaurants. It is a local historic landmark.

Go west on Ninth Avenue South. On the left is the Jordan Park Community Center/Woodson Museum.

4 Jordan Park Community Center/Woodson Museum

2240 9th Ave. S

Today this building serves as the Woodson African American Museum of Florida. It began its life as the community center for the Jordan Park housing complex. It was the launching point of

the 1968 Sanitation Workers' Strike, a 116-day strike for better pay and working conditions for the city's 211 sanitation workers. Strikers marched to City Hall from here more than 40 times. It is a local historic landmark.

Continue west on Ninth Avenue South. On the left is the Jordan Elementary.

5 Jordan Elementary

2390 9th Ave. S

Jordan Academy (later Jordan Elementary) was built in 1925 as the second Black elementary school in St.

Petersburg. The school quickly became overcrowded, serving 1,100 children by 1927. Jordan Elementary closed in 1975. It is a local historic landmark and houses a Head Start program.

Return to 22nd Street and turn right. Before 11th Avenue South, you'll come upon the Royal Theater.

6 Royal Theater

1011 22nd St. S

Built in 1948, the Royal Theater was one of two movie theaters that African Americans could attend, the other being the Harlem Theater in the Gas Plant neighborhood. The theater housed 700 seats and had a marching band on opening day. Its Quonset-style design was popular after World War II. It closed in 1966 and was renovated in 2004 as a Boys and Girls Club, with funding contributed by Hollywood star Angela Bassett, who grew up in nearby Jordan Park. It is a local historic landmark.

Continue south. Just past St. Petersburg College is the former Mercy Hospital.

ST. PETERSBURG MUSEUM OF HISTORY

7 Mercy Hospital
1344 22nd St. S

Mercy Hospital, the official city hospital for African Americans, opened at this location in 1923. It was staffed by a series of influential Black physicians like Dr. James Ponder and Dr. Fred Alsup, and dedicated nurses who made the best of the hospital's limited resources. It closed in 1966 and later reopened as the Johnnie Ruth Clarke Center. It is a local historic landmark.

A block and a half south, on the northwest corner of 22nd Street and 15th Avenue South, is the Ralph Wimbish Doctor's Office and Apartments.

8 Ralph Wimbish Doctor's Office and Apartments
1427 22nd St. S and 1417–1421 22nd St. S

Dr. Ralph Wimbish built his doctor's office on the corner here in 1955, and next to it, a two-story apartment building (you can still see the name Wimbish on the top floor). Doctor's Pharmacy, the first Black-owned pharmacy in St. Petersburg, operated here. Dr. Wimbish, and his wife, C. Bette Wimbish were leading civil rights activists in the city, and Mrs. Wimbish would become the first African American elected to St. Petersburg's city council.

MONICA KILE

On the southwest side of 15th Avenue and 22nd Street you'll find the Robert Swain Dental Office and Apartments.

9 Robert Swain Dental Office and Apartments
1501 22nd St. S (dental office) and 1511 22nd St. S (apartments)

Born in St. Petersburg, Dr. Robert Swain graduated from Howard University's dental school, served in World War II, and began practicing dentistry in 1947. His plans to build an office here in 1954 were initially denied because it was beyond the dividing line between Black and White neighborhoods. The city reversed its decision when Swain threatened to sue.

Swain built the apartments in 1956 to host Black travelers not allowed at White hotels. Olympic star Jesse Owens; baseball players Elston Howard, Bill White, and Roberto Clemente; and tennis star Althea Gibson all stayed here. In 1961, Dr. Swain and Dr. Ralph Wimbish provided the catalyst for the desegregation of spring training by refusing to continue housing Black baseball players. The buildings are local historic landmarks.

MONICA KILE

There are additional important historic sites along Ninth Avenue South, east of 22nd Street. Use the African American Heritage Trail signs as your guide to the churches, Happy Workers Nursery, and Fannye Ayer Ponder Clubhouse.

ACKNOWLEDGMENTS

This book wouldn't have been possible without the help of many people. I'd like to thank the staff at Reedy Press for their guidance and patience. I am so grateful to my friend Dexter Fabian, owner of I Love the Burg, who humored my idea of creating virtual tours during the pandemic, and who continues to give me a platform on which to write about beautiful buildings and conduct historic walking tours. Dex is a gift to our city. Tombolo Bookstore owners Alsace and Candice have created an inviting space for people who love to read, and it was Candice who steered me toward a walking-tour book when she told me that people always came into the store looking for maps of the area.

I wouldn't be in St. Petersburg if not for my cousin, the vaunted historian Raymond O. Arsenault. He lured me down for the Florida Studies Program and then introduced me to Peter Belmont, who became one of my best friends and mentors on how to advocate for and celebrate historic buildings and places. Likewise, Emily Elwyn leaves me in awe of her knowledge of historic architecture and her tireless devotion to saving old buildings (and she saved me from some factual mistakes in this book).

My dear friend Louise Diesbrock has always made me feel that, despite my many flaws, I am a special and talented person. She offers the wisest and most constructive criticism of my writing. The Forerunners running group has heard more than their fair share of my opinions on historic buildings (and every other topic), and the Minichillo family has indulged me in many a historic adventure (and Heather was the final reader).

My mom Peggy instilled in me a love of reading and travel, while my dad Duane passed on his love of history; for both I am eternally grateful.

My poor children, James and Anna, have been dragged around St. Petersburg, and many other cities across the world, in the pursuit of cool history. They coined the term "mommy miles" to describe the many walks that were supposed to be "just a mile or two" and ended up much longer so that we could check out the next interesting block. But now they're the most interesting kids I know and my joy in life.

Last, but most certainly not least, I'd like to thank my husband, Jon Kile, without whom this book would not exist. His love is the greatest gift I have ever received, and his wit brightens every one of my days. As the Avett Brothers say, "Always remember there is nothing worth sharing like the love that let us share our name."

SOURCES

Books

Arsenault, Raymond. *St. Petersburg and the Florida Dream, 1888–1950.* Gainesville, FL: University Press of Florida, 1996.

Ayers, R. Wayne. *Images of America: St. Petersburg, the Sunshine City.* Charleston, SC: Arcadia Publishing, 2001.

Baker, Rick. *Mangroves to Major League: A Timeline of St. Petersburg, Florida.* St. Petersburg, FL: Southern Heritage Press, 2000.

Baker, Rick. *The Seamless City: A Conservative Mayor's Guide to Urban Revitalization That Can Work.* Washington, DC: Regnery Publishing, 2011.

Bethell, John A. Pinellas: *A Brief History of the Lower Point.* St. Petersburg, FL: Press of the Independent Job Department, 1914.

Breslaur, Ken. *Historic Sites and Architecture of St. Petersburg, Florida.* Denver, CO: Outskirts Press, Inc., 2011.

Deese, Alma Wynelle. *St. Petersburg: Past and Present.* Atglen, PA: Schiffer Publishing LTD, 2008.

Dunn, Hampton. *Yesterday's St. Petersburg.* Miami, FL: E.A. Seeman Publishing, Inc. 1973.

Grismer, Karl H. *History of St. Petersburg: Historical and Biographical.* St. Petersburg, FL: Tourist News Publishing Company, 1924.

Hartzell, Scott Taylor. *Remembering St. Petersburg, Florida.* Charleston, SC: History Press, 2006.

Hartzell, Scott Taylor. *Remembering St. Petersburg, Florida, Volume 2, More Sunshine City Stories.* Charleston, SC: History Press, 2006.

Hartzell, Scott Taylor. *Voices of America: St. Petersburg, an Oral History.* Charleston, SC: Arcadia Publishing, 2002.

Michaels, Will. *The Making of St. Petersburg.* Charleston, SC: History Press, 2012.

Michaels, Will. *Hidden History of St. Petersburg.* Charleston, SC: History Press, 2016.

Mormino, Gary R. *Land of Sunshine, State of Dreams: A Social History of Modern Florida.* Gainesville, FL: University Press of Florida, 2005.

Peck, Rosalie and Jon Wilson. *St. Petersburg's Historic 22nd Street South.* Charleston, SC: History Press, 2006.

Peck, Rosalie and Jon Wilson. *St. Petersburg's Historic African American Neighborhoods.* Charleston, SC: History Press, 2008.

Rooks, Sandra W. *St. Petersburg Florida [Black America Series].* Charleston, SC: Arcadia Press, 2003.

Schnur, James Anthony. *St. Petersburg through Time.* Stroud, Gloucestershire, UK: Fonthill Media, 2014.

Sitler, Nevin D. *Warm Wishes from Sunny St. Pete: The Success Story of Promoting the Sunshine City.* Charleston: The History Press, 2014.

Wilson, Jon. *The Golden Era in St. Petersburg: Postwar Prosperity in the Sunshine City.* Charleston: The History Press, 2013.

Pamphlet/Booklet

Preserve the 'Burg. Historic St. Petersburg: Self-Guided Tour. St. Petersburg, 2020.

Newspapers

Tampa Bay Times/St. Petersburg Times. Accessible through Newspapers.com

The Weekly Challenger (St. Petersburg). Digital Newspaper Archive and Research Guide. https://lib.stpetersburg.usf.edu/weeklychallenger

Digital Library Archives and Resources

Burgert Brothers Photographic Collection. https://hcplc.org/research/burgert. A digital project of the Tampa-Hillsborough County Public Library System.

Florida Memory: Florida Photographic Collection. https://www.floridamemory.com/photographiccollection.

Sanborn Maps of Florida. Sanborn Fire Insurance Company. University of Florida Digital Collections. https://ufdc.ufl.edu/collections/sanborn.

Digital Commons @ University of South Florida. https://digitalcommons.usf.edu. Earl R. Jacobs III Collection of Francis G. Wagner's St. Petersburg Photographs. USF St. Petersburg Library. https://digitalcommons.usf.edu/wagner.

St. Petersburg Museum of History. http://spmoh.com.

"City of St. Petersburg Mayor's Historic Preservation Summit." City of St. Petersburg, June 24, 2006. https://bit.ly/3ccRkoQ.

Historic Preservation Interactive Map. City of St. Petersburg. https://bit.ly/2Y781uG.

INDEX